EXTREME SENSES
ANIMALS WITH UNUSUAL SENSES FOR HUNTING PREY

written by Kathryn Lay
illustrated by Christina Wald

magic
wagon

visit us at www.abdopublishing.com

Published by Magic Wagon, a division of the ABDO Group, PO Box 398166, Minneapolis, MN 55439.
Copyright © 2013 by Abdo Consulting Group, Inc. International copyrights reserved in all countries. All rights reserved. No part of this book may be reproduced in any form without written permission from the publisher.

Looking Glass Library™ is a trademark and logo of Magic Wagon.

Printed in the United States of America, North Mankato, Minnesota.
052012
092012
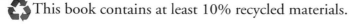This book contains at least 10% recycled materials.

Written by Kathryn Lay
Illustrated by Christina Wald
Edited by Stephanie Hedlund and Rochelle Baltzer
Cover and interior layout and design by Neil Klinepier

Library of Congress Cataloging-in-Publication Data

Lay, Kathryn.
 Extreme senses : animals with unusual senses for hunting prey / written by Kathryn Lay ; illustrated by Christina Wald.
     p. cm. -- (Sensing their prey)
 Includes index.
 ISBN 978-1-61641-865-6
 1. Senses and sensation--Juvenile literature. 2. Animal behavior--Juvenile literature. I. Wald, Christina, ill. II. Title.
 QP434.L39 2013
 612.8--dc23
                          2011052622

CONTENTS

Extreme Senses

Animals use their senses to find food. Many animals use their strong senses of touch, taste, smell, hearing, and sight. But others have different, unusual senses that help them find their prey.

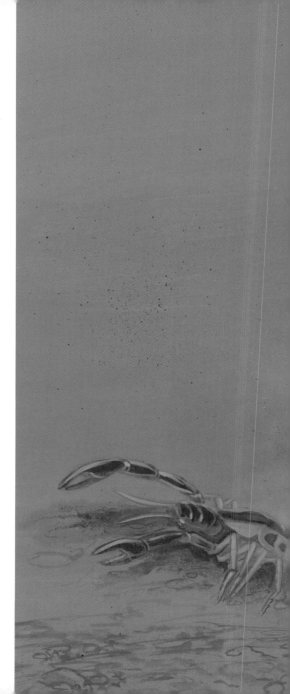

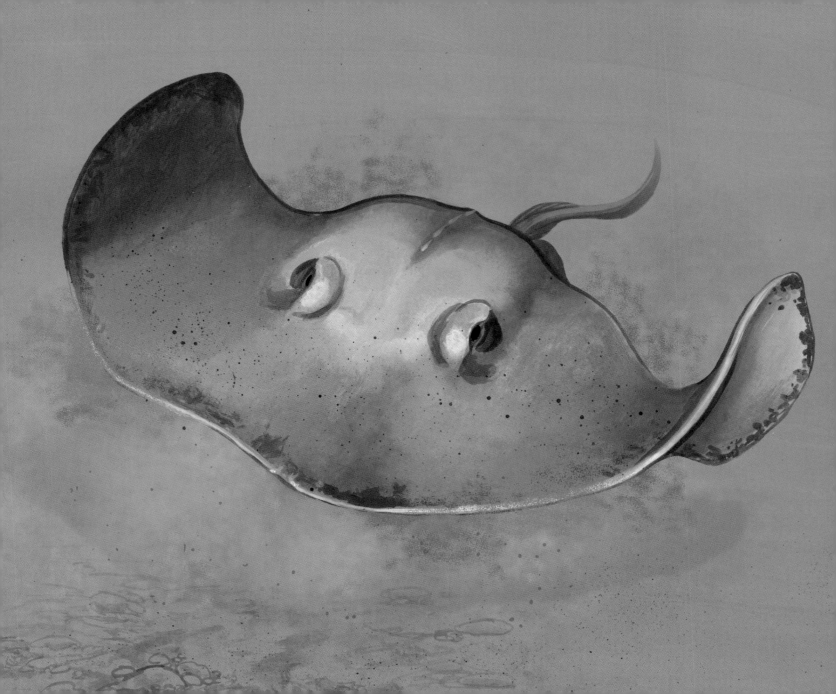

Echolocation

Bats use a sense called echolocation to find their way around in the dark. They also use this sense to locate their food. Echolocation is a process for locating distant or unseen objects by using sound waves.

Bats send out sound waves that they create from their mouth or nose. When the sound goes out, it hits an object. Then, an echo bounces back to the bat. The bat uses the echo to identify the object's location, size, shape, and texture.

If you yell in the kitchen when it is dark, do you feel sound bouncing off the refrigerator?

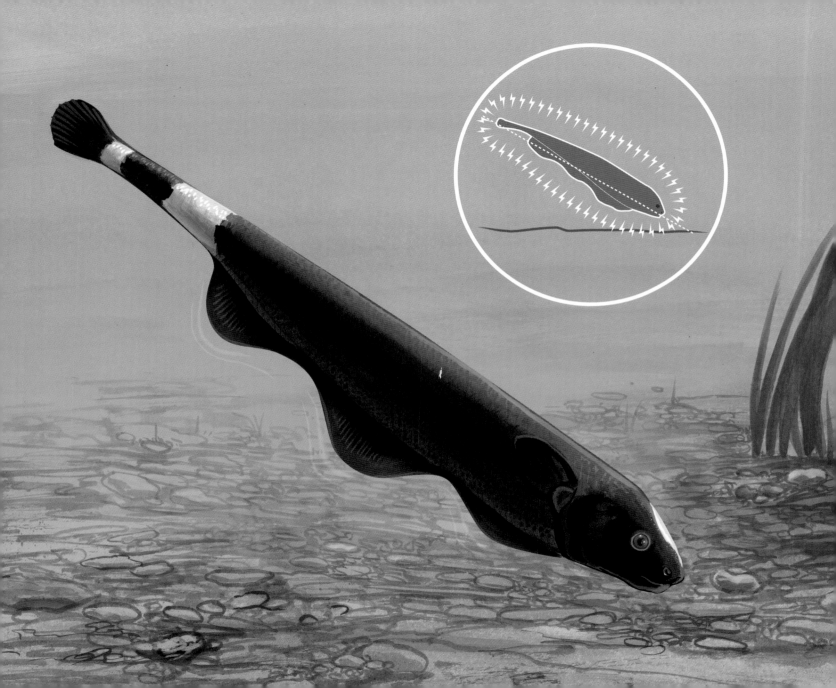

Bringing Prey to the Predator

The small, black ghost knifefish senses prey by sending out a weak electric field around its body. It hunts by swimming at an angle. That way, it can sense things in all directions.

The knifefish swims back and forth very quickly to catch its prey. When it detects food, a fin on its underside allows it to suddenly slow and change direction to follow its prey.

Do you have to move back and forth quickly to get food? How many extreme senses do you have?

SENSING THE PREY'S HEART

The great white shark has eight senses. It can see, smell, touch, taste, hear, and sense water pressure and temperature. The eighth sense is detecting electrical charges in a fish's heart. It is able to sense a beating heart at long distances.

Pretend you are a great white shark hunting. Can you sense electrical charges around you?

Sensing Water Pressure

The Texas blind salamander searches the bottom of caves for food. It moves its head from side to side as it hunts. This creates water pressure waves around its prey. The waves let the salamander find its food.

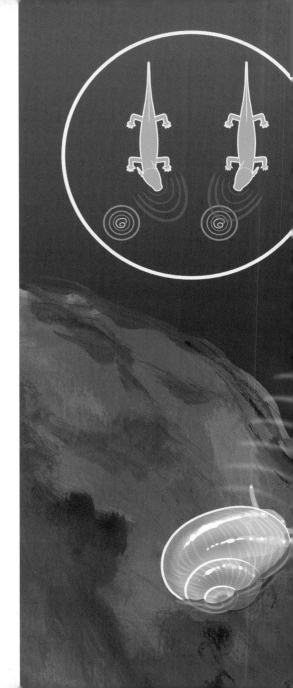

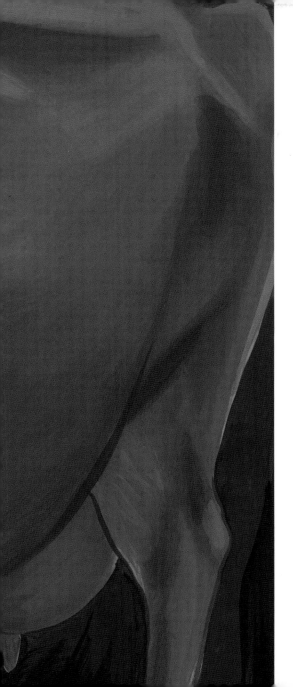

REMEMBERING THEIR PREY

The vampire bat remembers the sound of each victim's breath. It uses its memory to listen for the same animal when it wants to feed again.

The vampire bat identifies sounds in the same way that humans use their voices to recognize each other.

Vampire bats also sense heat to find prey. They have special organs around the nose and lips that sense heat and guide them to an animal.

Sensing with Their Mouth

The sunshine peacock cichlid fish hovers over the sand. It senses its prey just below the surface with its mouth. It uses its jaws as a sonar sensor.

When the prey is found, the fish darts its mouth into the sand. It sifts the sand through its gills while eating its food.

NOSE TENTACLES

The star-nosed mole is found in Canada and North America. Its nose is hairless. It is ringed by a unique "star" of 22 pink, fleshy tentacles. These tentacles are very sensitive to touch and electrical impulses.

The star-nosed mole finds its prey without sight. It uses its supersensitive tentacles to identify prey in under half a second! Star-nosed moles feed on insects, crustaceans, and earthworms.

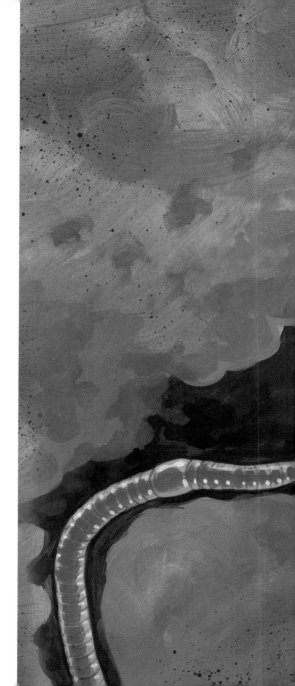

An Electrifying Sense

Stingrays hunt by sensing their prey's electricity. They use electrical sensing to detect prey buried in the sandy ocean bottom.

Amazing Senses

Even without sight, smell, or hearing, many predators are able to find food. Do you sense your stomach growling? Maybe you are hungry, too!

Glossary

crustacean - any of a group of animals with hard shells that live mostly in water. Crabs, lobsters, and shrimp are all crustaceans.

electric - something that uses electricity.

impulse - an electrical charge that causes a body to do something.

sonar - a device for detecting the presence and location of objects by using sound waves.

sound wave - sound vibrations that move through air with a motion like a wave in water.

tentacle - a long, slender body part that grows around the mouth or the head of some animals.

texture - the look and feel of something.

unique - being the only one of its kind.

victim - a person or animal that has been hurt.

Index

Web Sites

To learn more about animal senses, visit ABDO Group online at **www.abdopublishing.com**. Web sites about animal senses are featured on our Book Links page. These links are routinely monitored and updated to provide the most current information available.